Abingdon's
Bible Brain Teasers

ISBN 0-687-093244

Writer/Editor: LeeDell Stickler
Production Editor: Lucinda Anderson
Production and Design Manager:
R.E. Osborne
Designer: Paige Easter
Cover: Paige Easter
Illustrator: Megan Jeffery

01 02 03 04 05 06 07 08 09 10—10 9 8 7 6 5 4 3 2 1
MANUFACTURED IN THE UNITED STATES OF AMERICA

TABLE OF CONTENTS

1 CORINTHIANS: 3:16

Bible Brain Teasers

TABLE OF CONTENTS CONTINUED

THE NAMING

Answers on: pg. 64

lion

God told Adam to name all the animals.
What name did Adam give to each of these animals?

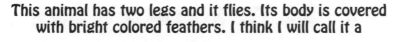

This animal looks like a bandit because it always wearing a mask. I think I will call it a _____.

This animal has a long mane and a loud roar. I think I will call it a _____.

spider

This animal lives in the forest, eats honey, and sleeps during the winter. I think I will call it a _____.

bat

snake

This animal has no legs but can move very fast. I makes a sound to warn you to "beware." I think I will call it a _____.

This animal has two legs and it flies. Its body is covered with bright colored feathers. I think I will call it a _____.

whale

turtle

This animal has four legs and carries its house around on its back. I think I will call it a _____.

This animal has four legs and a very long neck. I think I will call it a _____.

parrot

giraffe

This animal has eight legs and lives in the water. It moves about by squirting jets of water. I think I will call it an _____.

raccoon

This animal has eight legs. It spins a web to catch its dinner. I think I will call it a _____.

fish

This animal has no legs at all and lives in the water. I think I will call it a _____.

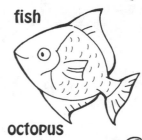

This animal has two legs and wings, but it isn't a bird. It likes to hunt for its dinner at night. I think I will call it a _____.

octopus

bear

This animal has no legs and lives in the water. But it isn't a fish. I think I will call it a _____.

GOD'S SPECIAL GARDEN

Answers on: pg. 64

Mark out all the Xs. Mark out all the Ys. Mark out all the Zs. Mark out all the Qs. Mark out all the K's. Mark out all the Bs.
The letters that are left will spell out the name of God's special Garden.

Z G K X Q Y Z Q
Q Y A Z Y K X K
Y O Q R Z B Q X
X X F X D Z X B
B E Q Z K E Y Z
K N D Y Q X N Y
Q Z B E Z B Q X
Z Y Q X N K Z Y

GENESIS 2:4–16

Bible Brain Teasers

JUNGLE JUMBLE

Answers on: pg. 64

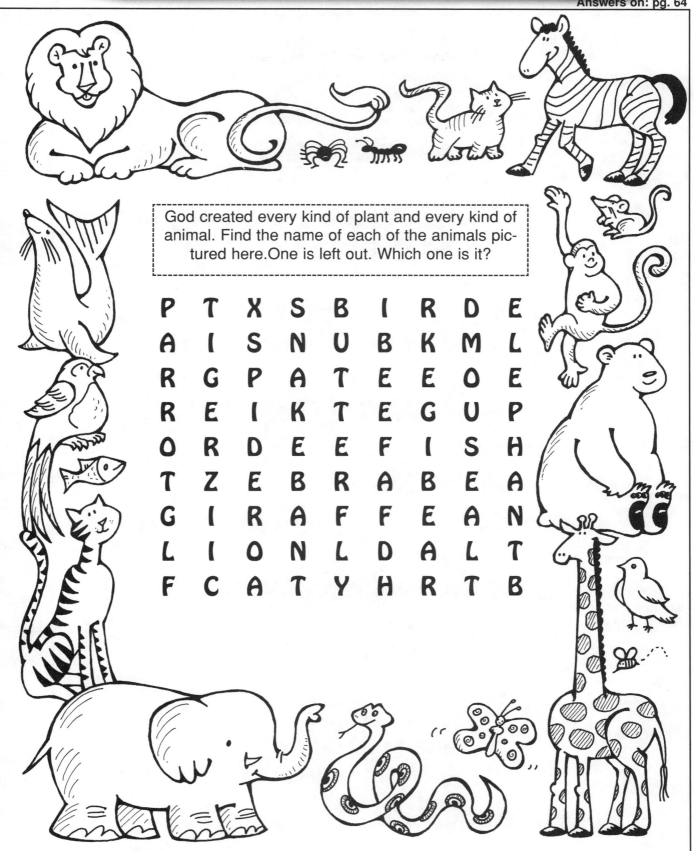

God created every kind of plant and every kind of animal. Find the name of each of the animals pictured here. One is left out. Which one is it?

```
P  T  X  S  B  I  R  D  E
A  I  S  N  U  B  K  M  L
R  G  P  A  T  E  E  O  E
R  E  I  K  T  E  G  U  P
O  R  D  E  E  F  I  S  H
T  Z  E  B  R  A  B  E  A
G  I  R  A  F  F  E  A  N
L  I  O  N  L  D  A  L  T
F  C  A  T  Y  H  R  T  B
```

GENESIS 1:20–25

Bible Brain Teasers

7

A SPECIAL SIGN

Noah sent out an animal to see if the waters from the flood had gone down. What animal did he send out?

74

73

72

65

75

1 ★

2

71

66

8

3

70

67

64

69

9

7

68

4

6

63

5

61

62

54

53

60

59

10

58

55

13

52

14

15

57

20

51

50

16

56

11

17

46

49

12

21

19

45

23

43

44

47

24

18

48

25

22

31

26

29

42

30

27

34

32

37

35

33

39

41

28

36

40

38

GOD'S PROMISE TO ABRAHAM

Answers on: pg. 64

Use the star code to discover the promise God made to Abraham.

A   E   H   I   L   N   R   T

C o u __ __ __ __ __

s __ __ __ s.

Y o u __ f __ m __ __ y

w __ __ __ b __

__ v __ __ __

g __ __ __ __ __ __

__ __ __ __ __ __ __ s __.

JOSEPH'S SPECIAL COAT

Of all his twelve sons, Joseph was Jacob's favorite.
Jacob gave Joseph a special long-sleeved coat.
Decorate Joseph's coat.

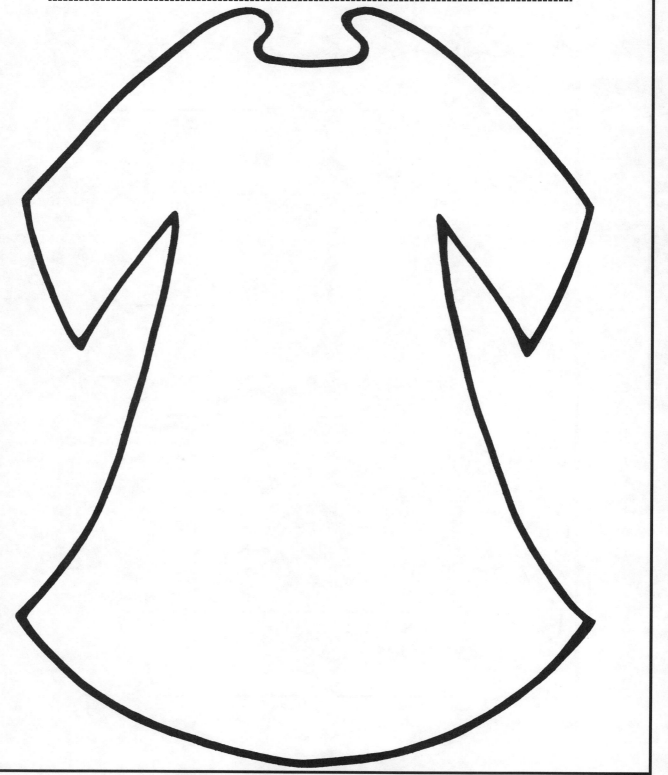

GENESIS 37:1–12

Bible Brain Teasers

JOSEPH IN EGYPT

Answers on: pg. 64

Joseph's brothers sold Joseph to a caravan of traders. The traders took Joseph to Egypt. Discover what Joseph learned.

1. Cut out the code strip on the far left.

2. Cut out the Egyptian mummy. Cut the slits on either side of the tablet the mummy is holding.

3. Punch holes as shown on the tablet.

4. Thread the code strip down through the slit on the left and up through the slit on the right. A letter will show in one of the holes; an hieroglyphic symbol will show in the other.

5. Slide the strip back and forth to solve the codes.

MESSAGE #1

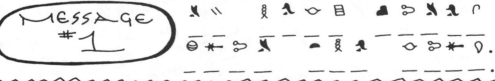

MESSAGE #2

MESSAGE #3

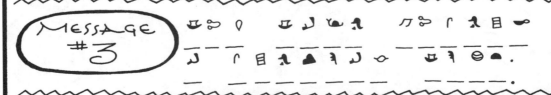

GENESIS 37:12–28

Bible Brain Teasers

A TRICKY BROTHER

Joseph's brothers thought they would never see their brother again. But they were wrong. Cut out the puzzle pieces. Put them together. Which one is Joseph?

GENESIS 42:1–25

Bible Brain Teasers

THE STORY OF MOSES

Answers on: pg. 64

Can you find the mistakes? Mark out the wrong word and write the correct word on the line.

Jochebed protected baby Moses by putting him in a box. _____

Moses' brother hid in the bushes and watched over him. _____

The Pharaoh's son saw the little basket in the river._____

When the princess opened the basket she found a puppy._____

Miriam went home to get her teacher to take care of the baby._____

The princess named the baby 'Moses' because it means "drawn from the cake batter."
_____

Moses' mother brought him to the king's daughter who raised him as her servant.

_____

Moses led his people out of slavery in New York._____

EXODUS 2:1–10

Bible Brain Teasers

MIX-UP AT THE OASIS

Water in the wilderness is rare. The people have gathered at the oasis for a drink. But something is wrong. Some of the people and objects reflected in the pool of water are not really there. Find all the mistakes.

EXODUS 15:22–27

Bible Brain Teasers

GOD'S TOP TEN

Answers on: pg. 64

Two letters are missing in this puzzle. Can you find them? Fill in the blanks, then read the group of laws that God gave the Hebrew people.

G __ d is the __ nly
G __ d.

W __ rship __ nly G __ d.

D __ n't use G __ d's
n __ me in __ b __ d
w __ y.

Keep the S __ bb __ th
d __ y h __ ly.

H __ n __ r y __ ur
f __ ther __ nd
m __ ther.

D __ n __ t c __ mmit
murder.

Be f __ ithful t __
y __ ur husb __ nd
__ r wife.

D __ n __ t ste __ l.

D __ n __ t tell lies.

D __ n __ t w __ nt
wh __ t bel __ ngs
t __ s __ me __ ne else.

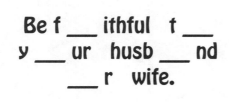

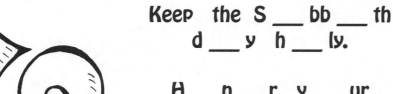

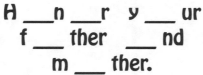

EXODUS 20:1–19

The Shema was written on a parchment scroll and placed inside a special box called a mezuzah. The mezuzah was placed on the doorpost of a house where family members would pass by. It reminded them to put God first in their lives. Make your own mezuzah.

Hear, O Israel: The LORD is our God, the LORD alone. You shall love the LORD your God with all your heart, and with all your soul, and with all your might.

Deuteronomy 6:4–5

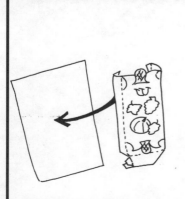

1. Color the mezuzah. Then cut it out.
2. Use a 3" x 5" note card or cut out a piece of posterboard that size.
3. Fold on the dotted lines.
4. Glue to card stock or posterboard as shown here.
5. Cut out the Bible verse. Roll the verse into a scroll. Place it inside the mezuzah.
6. Place your mezuzah in a spot where you will pass it every day.

SAMUEL'S NEW COAT

From the time Samuel was a boy he lived at the temple, helping Eli. Every year Hannah, Samuel's mother, would make him a new coat and bring it to the temple. Design Samuel's new coat.

1 SAMUEL 2:18–21

Bible Brain Teasers

DAVID'S SHIELD

David, the shepherd boy, became a soldier for King Saul.
He carried a sword and shield. Design a special shield for David.

I SAMUEL 18:1–9

Bible Brain Teasers

ELIJAH AND THE BOTTOMLESS JAR

Answers on: pg. 64

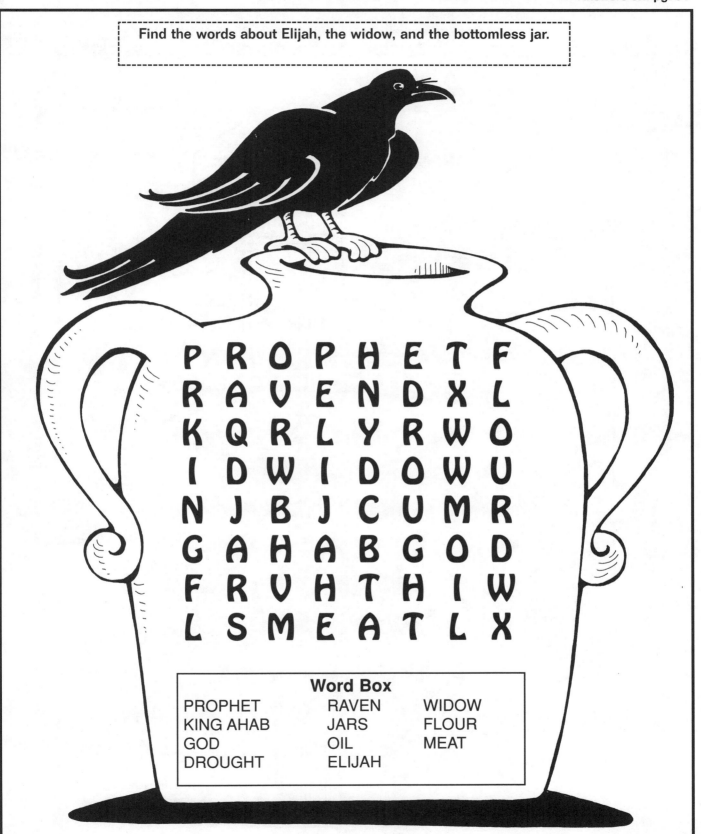

Find the words about Elijah, the widow, and the bottomless jar.

```
P  R  O  P  H  E  T  F
R  A  V  E  N  D  X  L
K  Q  R  L  Y  R  W  O
I  D  W  I  D  O  W  U
N  J  B  J  C  U  M  R
G  A  H  A  B  G  O  D
F  R  V  H  T  H  I  W
L  S  M  E  A  T  L  X
```

Word Box

PROPHET	RAVEN	WIDOW
KING AHAB	JARS	FLOUR
GOD	OIL	MEAT
DROUGHT	ELIJAH	

1 KINGS 17:1–24

JILLIONS OF JARS

Answers on: pg. 64

The prophet Elisha tells a widow to pour her small amount of oil into as many jars as she can gather. How many jars can you find?

2 KINGS 4:1-7

Bible Brain Teasers

JOSIAH AND THE HIDDEN SCROLLS

Answers on: pg. 64

When Josiah became king, he discovered that the Temple was in great need of repair.
During the repairs, a worker found clay jars that contained scrolls
that had not been read for many years. Which worker discovered the scrolls?

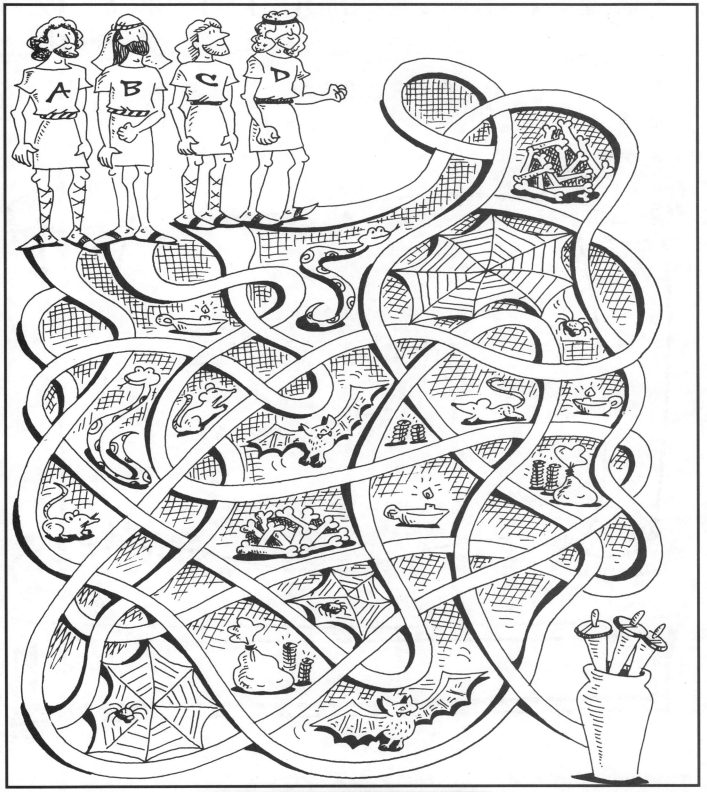

2 KINGS 22:1–24:5

Bible Brain Teasers

Answers on: pg. 64

Use the picture code. What does the psalmist tell us to do.?

PSALM 100

Bible Brain Teasers

The Book of Psalms has many poems and songs that praise God. Psalm 104 praises God as Creator.

Begin with the letter where the arrow is pointing. Follow the Bible verse by coloring each letter box as you go. You can color only those boxes that are touching on the sides, not the corners.

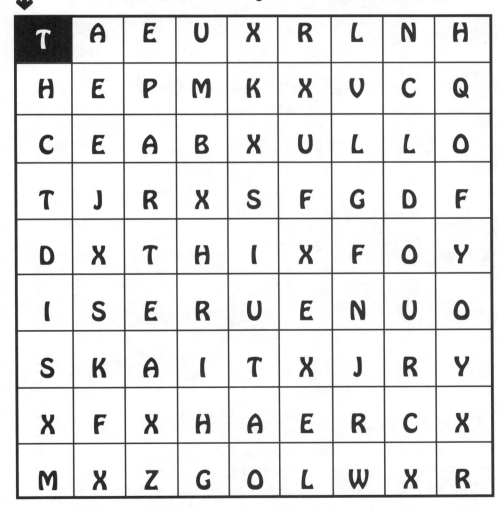

T	A	E	U	X	R	L	N	H
H	E	P	M	K	X	V	C	Q
C	E	A	B	X	U	L	L	O
T	J	R	X	S	F	G	D	F
D	X	T	H	I	X	F	O	Y
I	S	E	R	U	E	N	U	O
S	K	A	I	T	X	J	R	Y
X	F	X	H	A	E	R	C	X
M	X	Z	G	O	L	W	X	R

The earth is full of your creatures.
Psalm 104:24

A SPECIAL TREASURE

> **I will treasure your word in my heart. (Psalm 119:11, adapted)**
> Find the hidden coins that belong in the treasure chest.

PSALM 119:11

Bible Brain Teasers

FRIENDSHIP

A friend loves at all times. (Proverbs 17:17)
How many hearts can you find?

PROVERBS 17:17

Bible Brain Teasers

THE POTTER'S POTS

Answers on: pg.64

The potter has made many fine pots to sell.
However, in each row, one pot has a flaw.
Can you find it?

JEREMIAH 18:1-11

Bible Brain Teasers

DANIEL'S GOOD FOODS

Daniel and his friends were faithful and only ate only vegetables instead of the king's rich foods. Can you unscramble the names of the vegetables going into the chef's stew?

satoomte

snoion

ebset

rcno

tarosrc

aepotost

aspe

seepppr

nbase

sqhusa

babaegc

DANIEL AND THE LIONS DEN

Answers on: pg. 64

Find the words that tell about Daniel's adventure in the lion's den.
If you need help, look at the Word Box for hints.

```
A   B   Z   K   S   A   F   E   X   F
D   A   N   I   E   L   A   W   Y   A
V   B   H   N   J   I   K   W   P   I
I   Y   U   G   G   O   D   C   J   T
S   L   N   D   A   N   G   E   L   H
O   O   G   A   D   S   P   R   S   F
R   N   R   R   A   D   R   O   I   U
S   X   Y   I   L   E   A   O   G   L
K   Q   L   U   A   N   Y   M   N   Q
W   O   R   S   H   I   P   S   C   V
            M   O   L   U   A   H   E
                                Z
```

Word Box

Babylon
Daniel
King Darius
Advisors
Lions Den
Hungry
law
God
faithful
worship
palace
angel
pray
sign
law
safe
mouth
room

DANIEL 6
Bible Brain Teasers

A GIFT OF FOOD

Ruth picked up the grains of wheat the workers had left behind. This grain made bread for her and Naomi. Help those who are hungry each week by saving a portion of your allowance in this envelope. Then give the money to a food program.

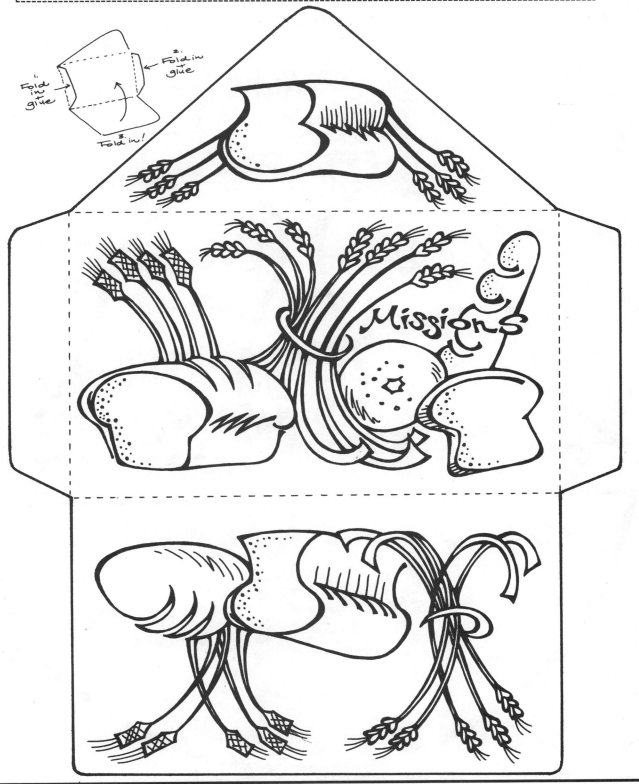

GOOD NEWS, MARY!

God sent the angel Gabriel to Mary to tell her the good news. Mary would be the mother of God's Son, Jesus. Make an angel ornament to hang on your Christmas tree.

Bring points A + B around to back and tape

Bring arms to the front and interlock.

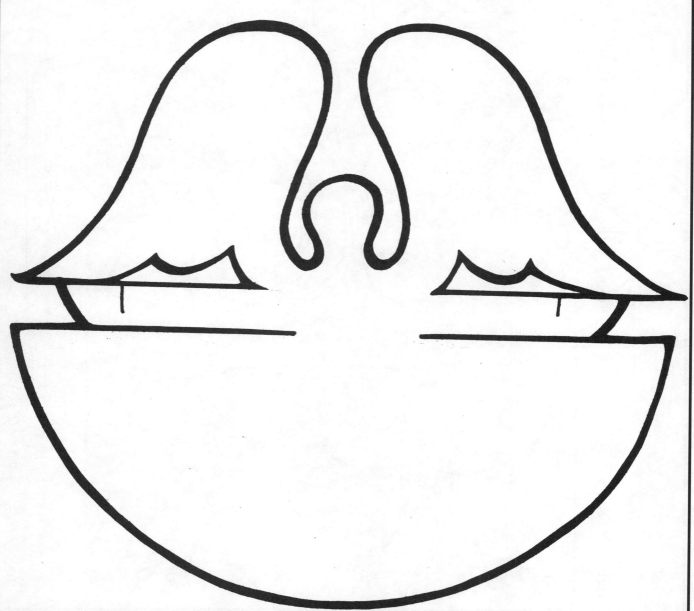

LUKE 1:26—38

Bible Brain Teasers

NO ROOM IN THE INN

Jesus, God's only Son, was born in a stable. Color the picture.

LUKE 2:1-7

Bible Brain Teasers

SHEPHERDS HEAR THE NEWS

Answers on: pg. 64

> What did the angels tell the shepherds? Read the Bible verse.
> Fill in the missing words.

Do not be _____.

For see, I am _____

you good _____ of great

_____ for all the _____.

To you is _____ this day in

the city of _____

a _____ who is the

_____the Lord.

LUKE 2:8–20

Bible Brain Teasers

A SPECIAL SIGN

Wise men from the east studied the heavens. One day they saw a sign that told them a new king had been born. What was this sign?

Color those spaces with a + yellow.
Color those spaces with a • black.

MATTHEW 2:1–12

Bible Brain Teasers

A MISSING BOY

When Jesus was twelve years old he traveled with his parents to the Temple for the Passover. When his parents started for home, however, Jesus stayed behind. Can you help Mary and Joseph find their missing son?

LUKE 2:42-52

Bible Brain Teasers

THE FISHERMEN

The first disciples Jesus called were fishermen on Lake Galilee.
How many fish can you find hidden in the picture?

MATTHEW 4:18–22

Bible Brain Teasers

THE TWELVE DISCIPLES

Answers on: pg. 64

Find the names of Jesus' twelve disciples. Then see how many times the word FISH is found in the puzzle.

```
P H I L I P Q W Z M K
E F I S H X J U D M K
T H A D D A E U S A S
E X F I S H F Z Q T X
R J A M E S Q J V H Z
B A R T H O L O M E K
J M X H Q Z F H V W W
F E X O K A Y N K I F
I S I M O N Y Q Z W I
S L V A N D R E W H S
H F I S H F I S H H Z
```

Peter, Andrew, James (Son of Alphaeus), James (Son of Zebedee), John, Bartholomew, Philip, Thaddaeus, Thomas, Judas, Matthew, Simon

MARK 3:16–19

Bible Brain Teasers

LEVI THE TAX COLLECTOR

Levi the tax collector wants to return the money he has stolen.
Help Levi find the missing coins.

LUKE 5:27–32

Bible Brain Teasers

37

PHILIP BRINGS A FRIEND

Answers on: pg. 64

Help Philip bring his friend Nathanael to meet Jesus. Then count to discover the number of boats, ducks, sheep, flowers and people.?

JOHN 1:43–51

Bible Brain Teasers

BLESSED ARE THE PEACEMAKERS

In the Beatitudes, Jesus told the people how they were to live in God's kingdom. Make a Beatitude Attitude hanging to remind you how to live in God's Kingdom.

Blessed are the Peacemakers, for they will be called children of God.
(Matthew 5:9)

1. Remove the center from a large white paper dinner plate.
2. Using the dove and hearts as patterns, cut several from red and white construction paper.
3. Write some of the ways you are to live in God's kingdom on each heart or dove.
4. Glue them around the plate.
5. Hang the Bible verse heart as shown.

Cut out center of paper plate

Glue on doves and hearts

BACK OF WREATH

Back of Bible Verse heart

Thread Bible Verse heart with yarn. Tape to back of wreath.

MATTHEW 5:1–10

FEEDING THE FIVE THOUSAND

One day Jesus fed a crowd of over 5000 people with a small boy's lunch—five loaves of barley bread and two fish. Can you find the leftover bread and fish?

JOHN 6:1–15

Bible Brain Teasers

JESUS HEALS

When Jesus healed the paralyzed man, he said something that amazed everyone.
What did Jesus tell the man? Color every space that is marked with a ●

MARK 2:1–12
Bible Brain Teasers

LET YOUR LIGHT SHINE

Tape this picture over a sheet of black construction paper. Using a push pin or a tooth-pick, punch out the dotted design. Remove the top sheet. Hold the black paper up to the light. When we live as Jesus taught, then we are letting our "love light" shine.

MATTHEW 5:13–16

Bible Brain Teasers

THE UNFORGIVING SERVANT

Cut out the storybook about the unforgiving servant.
Fold the book in half in the center along the dotted line.
Then fold in half again. Color the pictures. Share the story with a friend.

Matthew 18:23–35

Once there was a king . . .

The Unforgiving Servant

gives you.
Remember: Forgive others as God for-
debt was paid.
the servant arrested and put in jail until his
had. He was very angry. He had
When the king heard what the first ser-

The king forgave the man his debt and
sent him on his way. The man was so happy
he danced for joy.
As he left, the man ran into a friend who
owed him money. "Pay up or I will have you
put in jail," the man said.

One day he called together all persons
who owed him money.
"Pay me or go to jail," he said.
One man could not pay. He begged the
king. "Give me more time."

WHAT'S HAPPENING HERE?

Jesus told stories called parables to help people understand
what he was trying to teach. This picture tells about one of the stories Jesus told.
Connect the dots. What is happening here?

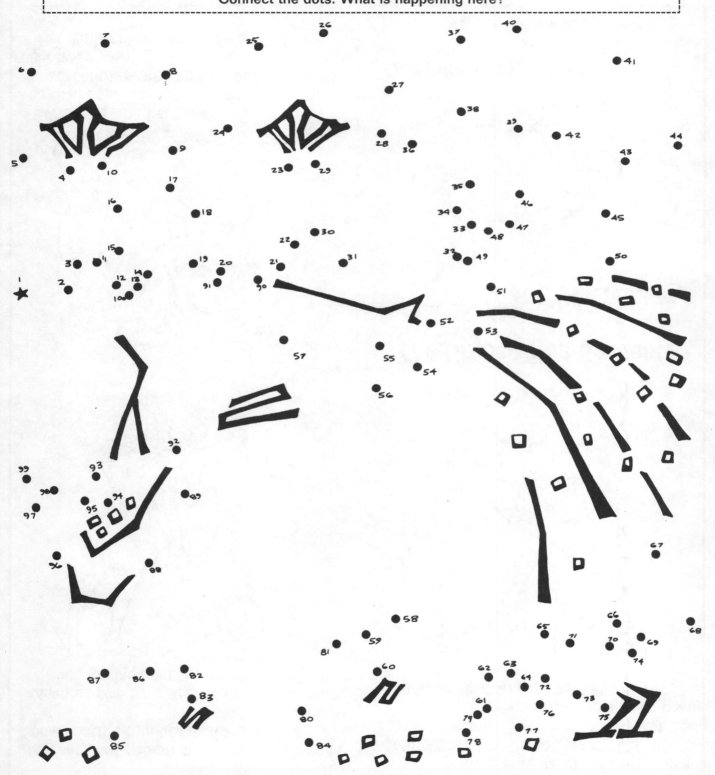

MATTHEW 13:1–9

Bible Brain Teasers

THE LOST SHEEP

Ninety-seven, ninety-eight, ninety-nine . . . One sheep is missing! Help the shepherd find his lost sheep.

LUKE 15:1–7

Bible Brain Teasers

THE FORGIVING FATHER

Answers on: pg. 64

Read the story of the Forgiving Father. What animal did the younger son have to take care of? When the younger son became discouraged, where did he go? Use the color code to find the answers

❑ = blue   ✗ = red   ☆ = yellow   ◯ = green   ✳ = purple

LUKE 15:11–32

Bible Brain Teasers

Each of these is an item that could be found inside a Bible times house.
Write the word in the matching space. Then write the circled letters in the spaces below.

broom

mill

spoon

basket

bowl

lamp

oven

spindle

stove

mattress

jar

mat

3   5   7   9   8   11   12

ZACCHAEUS THE TAX COLLECTOR

Zacchaeus was a tax collector. He worked for the Romans
When Zacchaeus met Jesus it changed his life forever.
Can you help the people get to Zacchaeus to pay their taxes?

Start→

Finish→

LUKE 19:1-11

Bible Brain Teasers

BLESSED IS THE ONE!

Help Jesus get from the city gate to the Temple.
See how many points you can collect along the way.

KEY:
Palm leaf = 1 point
cloak = 2 points

MATTHEW 21:1-11

Bible Brain Teasers

THE LAST SUPPER

Mark out all the Xs. Mark out all the As.
Mark out all the Zs. Mark out all the Ms.
Mark out all the Qs.
What did Jesus tell his friends that night at Passover?

```
Z  X  Q  M  Q  Z  X  X  Z  Z
X  D  X  X  X  X  Q  Z  X  M
A  X  A  Z  A  Q  A  Z  A  X
Q  X  X  M  X  M  M  Z  X  Q
X  Q  Z  M  X  X  A  M  A  X
A  T  X  X  X  X  I  Z  M  A
X  Z  M  Q  H  X  Q  X  Q  X
Z  X  X  X  Z  A  X  Q  A  X
A  Q  M  X  M  A  A  Z  S  X
A  X  I  X  X  A  X  Z  X  M
A  X  Z  M  O  A  A  N  A  Q
X  X  E  X  X  R  X  Y  X  X
M  M  X  M  X  X  A  X  M  X
O  X  A  Q  Z  Q  X  A  X  F
X  Q  Z  X  X  X  E  A  Q  X
```

_____

LUKE 22:14–23

Bible Brain Teasers

WHEN THE COCK CROWS THREE TIMES

Answers on: pg. 64

Use the graph code. Write the words on the line.
What did Peter say when asked about Jesus?

	A	B	C	D	E	F	G
1	you	swords	I	girl	the	fire	love
2	rooster	kept	supper	leave	tomb	follow	Jesus
3	women	not	shouts	are	kept	Peter	servant
4	boat	prison	disciple	bread	enter	talking	arrest
5	hands	cross	night	deny	know	do	small
6	about	Mary	amazed	man	angry	priest	look
7	king	John	told	rooster	run	soldiers	know

C1   F5   B3   G7   E1   D6

A1   D3   F4   A6

MARK 14:66–72

Bible Brain Teasers

Color the area outside the cross black. This reminds us of the
day Jesus died. Color the inside of the cross with
many bright colors. This will remind us that Jesus lives!
Then dip a cotton ball in baby oil and rub lightly over the
picture. Blot with paper towels. Hang in a sunny window.

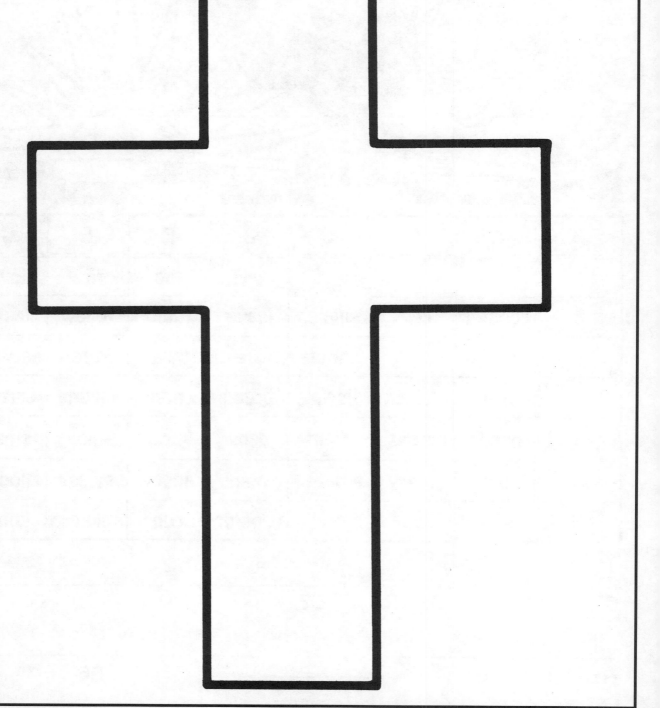

JOHN 19:17–27
Bible Brain Teasers

A SIGN OF NEW LIFE

Tear thumb-sized bits of colored tissue paper. Glue them onto the butterfly. Then trim around the outline. Place the butterfly in a sunny window.

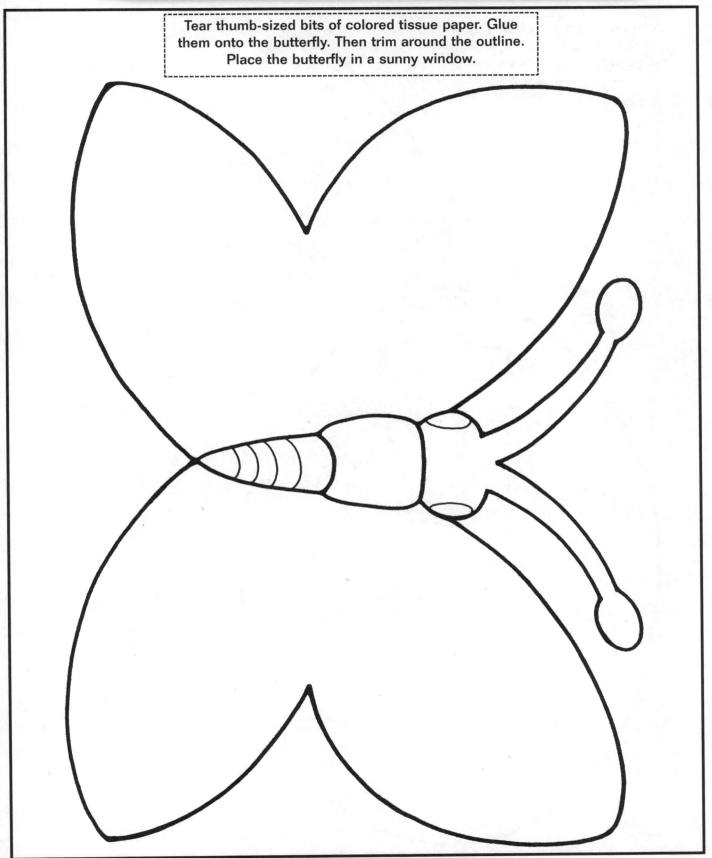

LUKE 24:1–12

Bible Brain Teasers

Color both sections of the Easter egg. Cut out both pieces. Join together with a paper fastener as shown.

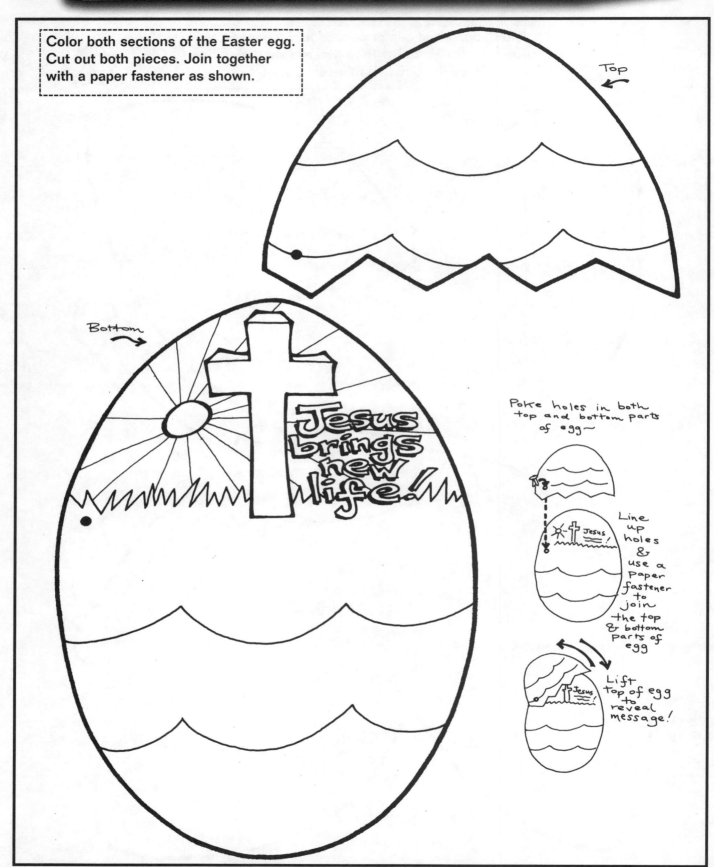

Top

Bottom

Poke holes in both top and bottom parts of egg~

Line up holes & use a paper fastener to join the top & bottom parts of egg

Lift top of egg to reveal message!

Jesus brings new life!

MATTHEW 28:1–9

Bible Brain Teasers

JESUS LIVES!

After his resurrection, Jesus appeared to seven of his disciples while they were fishing. Cut out the boxes at the bottom of the page. Finish the picture.

JOHN 21:1-14

Bible Brain Teasers

ALL ABOUT JESUS

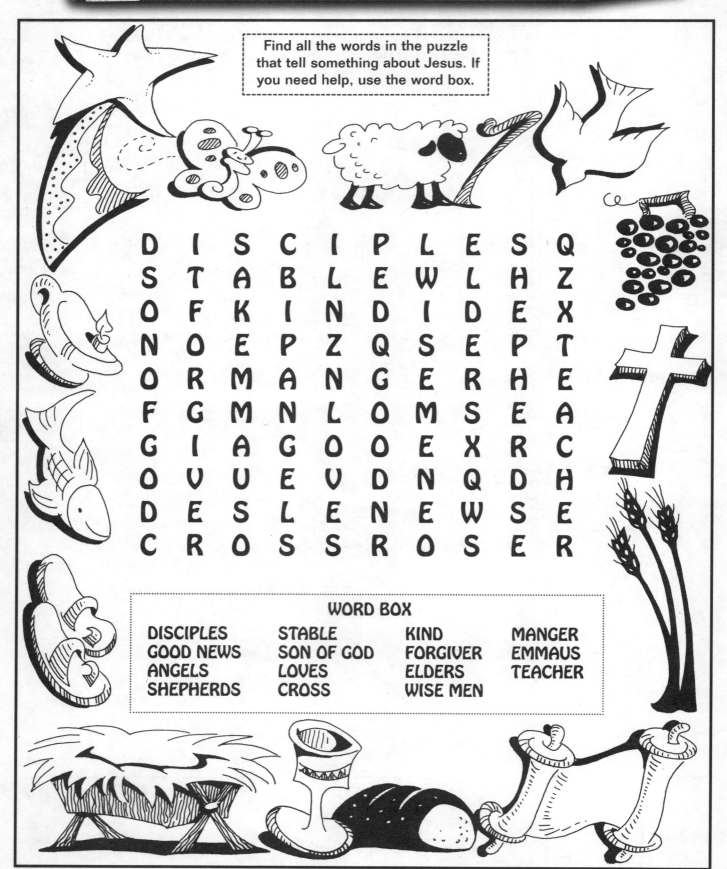

Find all the words in the puzzle that tell something about Jesus. If you need help, use the word box.

```
D  I  S  C  I  P  L  E  S  Q
S  T  A  B  L  E  W  L  H  Z
O  F  K  I  N  D  I  E  E  X
N  O  E  P  Z  Q  S  E  P  T
O  R  M  A  N  G  E  R  H  E
F  G  M  N  L  O  M  S  E  A
G  I  A  G  O  O  E  X  R  C
O  V  U  E  V  D  N  Q  D  H
D  E  S  L  E  N  E  W  S  E
C  R  O  S  S  R  O  S  E  R
```

WORD BOX

DISCIPLES	STABLE	KIND	MANGER
GOOD NEWS	SON OF GOD	FORGIVER	EMMAUS
ANGELS	LOVES	ELDERS	TEACHER
SHEPHERDS	CROSS	WISE MEN	

NEW TESTAMENT

Bible Brain Teasers

THE COMING OF THE HOLY SPIRIT

What did the disciples see in the room when the Holy Spirit came?
Color all the spaces with a ● black.
Color all the spaces with a ○ red.

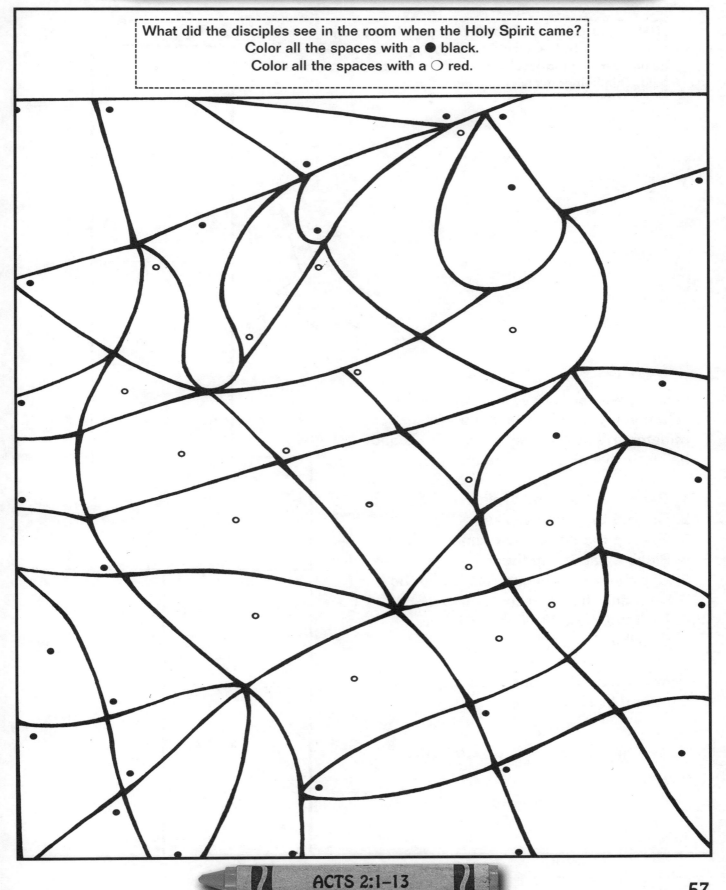

ACTS 2:1–13

Bible Brain Teasers

57

WITH WIND AND FLAME

Before Jesus left his disciples, he promised to send them a Helper. This Helper would come to them. This Helper would empower them to teach, and preach, and heal just as Jesus did. This helper is called the Holy Spirit.

Like air, we cannot see the Holy Spirit. When you play with the Wind Walker, remember that the Holy Spirit fills us and helps us live as Jesus taught.

1. Decorate the Wind Walker.
2. Cut out the Wind Walker.
3. Fold up the bottom two times.
4. Place a paper clip there.
5. Clip the top and bend one leg to the front and the other to the back.
6. Toss the Wind Walker as high as possible.

Watch the air catch the flaps and make the Wind Walker dance.

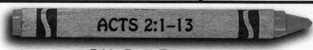

ACTS 2:1–13

Bible Brain Teasers

PAUL AND SILAS

Even when Paul and Silas were in jail, they praised God.
How many keys can you find to help them escape?
Read Acts 16:1–34. Find out what God did.

LOVE IS . . .

Paul wrote a letter to the church in Corinth telling them what love is. How many times can you find the word "love" in the square?

L O V E L O V E L O
O V E L O V E L O V
V E L O V E L O V E
E L O V E L O V E L
L O V E L O V E L O
O V E L O V E L O V
V E L O V E L O V E
E L O V E L O V E L
L O V E L O V E L O
O V E L O V E L O V
V E L O V E L O V E
E L O V E L O V E L
O V E L O V E L O V

1 CORINTHIANS 13:1–13

Bible Brain Teasers

WORKING TOGETHER AS CHRISTIANS

Let us work for the good of all. (Galatians 6:10)
Begin at the arrow. Collect the words from the Bible verse. Can you get to the center of the puzzle?

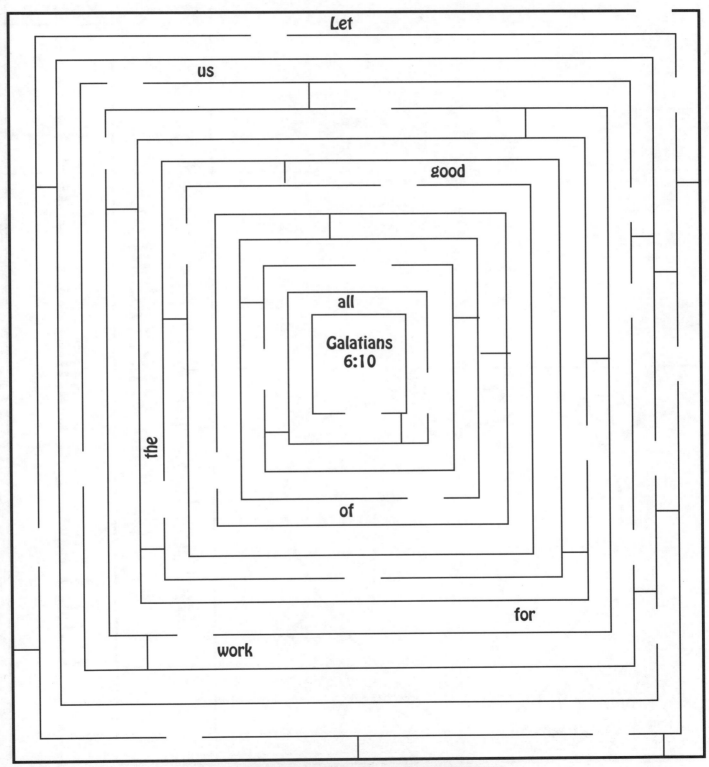

Let

us

good

all

Galatians
6:10

the

of

for

work

GOD IS LOVE

Cut out the heart card and the verse strips. Cut the two slits in the heart. Tape the verse strips together. Thread the strip up through the slit on the right and down through the slit on the left. Fold the card and glue around the bottom edge.

Glue here

We love because God first loved us. (1 John 4:19, (adapted)

Let us love one another. (1 John 4:7)

1 JOHN 4:7, 19

Bible Brain Teasers

PAUL AND LYDIA

Lydia was a cloth merchant from Philippi. She met Paul on the river bank. Paul told her about Jesus. Cut out the puppets of Paul and Lydia. Glue each puppet to the address-side of a business-sized envelope. Lick the flap and seal the envelope. Then cut off one end of the envelope (where the puppet's feet are). Slip your hand inside. Tell the story of Paul and Lydia.

ACTS 2:1–4

Bible Brain Teasers

Page 5: raccoon, lion, bear, rattlesnake, parrot, turtle, giraffe, octopus, spider, fish, bat, whale

Page 6: Garden of Eden

Page 7: monkey

Page 9: Count the stars. Your family will be even greater than these.

Page 11: Message #1—My help comes from the Lord; Message #2— God had a plan for Joseph; Message #3—God gave Joseph a special gift.

Page 12: Joseph is the one in the upper left corner.

Page 13: box/basket; brother/sister; son/daughter; puppy/baby; teacher/mother; cake batter/water; servant/son; New York/Egypt

Page 15: God is the only God. Worship only God. Don't use God's name in a bad way. Keep the sabbath day holy. Honor your father and mother. Do not commit murder. Be faithful to your husband or wife. Do not steal. Do not tell lies. Do not want what belongs to someone else.

Page 20: 10 jars

Page 21: Worker C found the scrolls.

Page 22: Worship the Lord with gladness.

Page 24: 11 coins

Page 25: 6 hearts

Page 26: Row 1—pot 5; Row 2—pot 2; Row 3—pot 4; Row 4—pot 1

Page 27: tomatoes, corn, peas, beans, cabbage, onions, potatoes, squash, peppers, carrots

Page 32: afraid, bringing, news, joy, people, born, David, Savior, Messiah

Page 35: 12 fish

Page 37: 14 coins

Page 38: 5 boats, 10 ducks, 5 trees, 17 sheep, 10 people

Page 40: 5 fish, 5 loaves of bread

Page 41: Your sins are forgiven.

Page 44: a sower

Page 46: pigs, home

Page 47: (1) jar, (2) lamp, (3) spoon, (4) oven, (5) basket, (6) stove, (7) mattress, (8) broom, (9) mat, (10) spindle, (11) mill, (12) bowl [Secret word—PARABLE]

Page 50: Do this in memory of me.

Page 51: I do not know the man you are talking about.

Page 57: flame

Page 59: 8 keys

Page 60: 50

Supplies

pencils	Bibles	white glue
felt-tip markers	paper fasteners	2 business-sized
crayons	tape	envelopes
scissors	stapler, staples	colored art tissue